Goat Funeral

Goat Funeral

poems by

Christopher Bakken

THE SHEEP MEADOW PRESS
RIVERDALE-ON-HUDSON, NEW YORK

All inquiries and permission requests should be addressed to:
The Sheep Meadow Press
P.O. Box 1345
Riverdale-on-Hudson, NY 10471

Designed and typeset by The Sheep Meadow Press.
Distributed by The University Press of New England.

Printed on acid-free paper in the United States. This book meets the guidelines for permanence and durability of the Committee on Production Guidelines for Book Longevity of the Council on Library Resources.

Library of Congress Cataloging-in-Publication Data
Bakken, Christopher, 1967-
 Goat funeral : poems / by Christopher Bakken.
    p. cm.
 ISBN 1-931357-43-9 (pbk. : acid-free paper)
 I. Title.

PS3602.A59G63 2006
811'.6—dc22

                                              2006017824

Acknowledgements

Grateful acknowledgement is made to the journals and anthologies where these poems first appeared:

Agni (online): "Portrait Detail, with Pear"

American Literary Review: "Anamnesis," "Eclogue 7 (Matia)"

The Gettysburg Review: "Days of 1987," "Theme Song for an Agrarian Epic"

Lyric: "Amanita muscaria," "Eclogue," "Eclogue 2"

Mare Nostrum: "Eclogue 3," "Eclogue 4"

Mid-American Review: "Portrait Detail, with Bat"

The Mississippi Review: "First Objects," "Eclogue 6," "Eclogue 9"

North American Review: "Anatomy," "Parenthesis"

Parnassus: Poetry in Review: "Blues for Bill Matthews, Dead at 55"

PN Review (U.K.): "Duet with Fernando Pessoa," "Duet with Salvatore Quasimodo"

Raritan: "The World Reduced to One Thing"

Redivider: "Purgatory, A Postcard"

Southwest Review: "Azaleas," "Minimalist Eclogue"

The Atlanta Review: "Aegean: Flight 652," "Last Words for Elpenor"

The Paris Review: "Coleridge in Valletta"

The Texas Review: "Paul Celan"

Western Humanities Review: "Ariadne (Postscript)," "Eclogue 8 (Winter)"

Witness: "Late Adam Thinking"

"Ohio Elegy" appeared in *Poets Against the War*, edited by Sam Hamill. Nation Books, 2003.

"Duet with D.H. Lawrence" appeared in *Under the Rock Umbrella: Modern American Poets from 1951-1976*. Mercer University Press, 2006.

I am grateful to Allegheny College and the International Writers' and Translators' Center of Rhodes for the support I received while writing these poems. Thanks also to the friends and family members who have offered assistance and support, in particular those who helped me shape this book: Kerry Neville Bakken, Aliki Barnstone, Corey Marks, David Miller, Stanley Moss, Alan Michael Parker, and Titos Patrikios.

Contents

1.

Theme Song for an Agrarian Epic　　　　　3
Anamnesis　　　　　5

2.

Eclogue　　　　　9
Eclogue 2　　　　　11
Eclogue 3 (Cyclops)　　　　　12
Eclogue 4 (Goat Funeral)　　　　　13
Eclogue 5　　　　　14
Eclogue 6　　　　　16
Minimalist Eclogue　　　　　17
Eclogue 7 (Matia)　　　　　18
Eclogue 8 (Winter)　　　　　19
Eclogue 9　　　　　20
Epode　　　　　22

3.

Days of 1987　　　　　25
The Blue Jay　　　　　26
Amanita muscaria　　　　　28
Anatomy　　　　　29
Portrait Detail, with Pear　　　　　32
Portrait Detail, with Bat　　　　　33
The World Reduced to One Thing　　　　　35

4.

Duet with Fernando Pessoa   39
Duet with Czeslaw Milosz   40
Duet with D. H. Lawrence   41
Blues for Bill Matthews, Dead at 55   42
Violin Solo   43
Parenthesis   44
Paul Celan   45
Duet with Salvatore Quasimodo   46

5.

Purgatory, a Postcard   49
Detail from *The Martyrdom of San Mauricio*, El Greco   50
Coleridge in Valletta   51
Azaleas   52
Late Adam Thinking   54
First Objects   55
Ohio Elegy   56
Ariadne (Postscript)   58
Last Words from Elpenor   59
Aegean: Flight 652   60

1.

Theme Song for an Agrarian Epic

for Eugene Meier

Our hero ruts the horizon. Hay gets made.
It's rained for two weeks straight
but the dead are back to sleep now.

Those who live must work. The garden
swarms with hornets and cabbage moths.
Sweet peas lay prostrate in the mud,

alchemizing raw sugar from the air.
There are only two sins here: sloth and wealth.
Even the kittens waste no time.

Yet, beneath the apple blossoms (you cannot
see her now) the farmer's daughter pouts
for love, ignores her reflection in the bird bath.

Do not ask her to speak.
Rotted poplars; a disheveled mane of willow.
The yawp of some mutt over the hill.

And always some scrap battered and rusting
behind the wobbly tool shed where
the hired help chuck what's not fit to fix.

High above the oats, a crow flying past
sees only the farmer's cap, red as a squashed tulip,
emblazoned with MOORMAN'S FEED.

Weary calves stagger home from their feast
of meadow-grass and dandelion. On the doorstep,
singing in the upper registers of cream,

one milk bottle gathers flies. You'll have enough.
The fields are full. The kitchen door
is always open, stranger. Go on in.

Anamnesis

for AB and RB

Era mi voz antigua
ignorante de los densos jugos amargos.
                    —Lorca

Sometime wade into the poppy-ditch,
          or cross inside the shade of icons,
at night when your back hurts, while you dream
          and both dogs gallop across fields they love,
then your body remembers, as I do.
          Sometime just a whiff of hay is enough.

Then, struck dumb by what returns,
          so lost it feels like pain, that past,
you'll see the child you were then:
          head broad as a pasture, much too bright,
before poetry, other disasters,
          how cold the air was that day you went down,

swallowed your tongue. Let's say the park
          (some bedraggled county acre) was
beautiful, though *beauty* wouldn't be
          a word we used back then: just three swings
and a rusted ladder you clamber too fast,
          bent on crashing the slide, bent

on breaking through the pit of sand. Each time
          your brother warns you, but the metal
thunders from your weight; you are a loud god,
          a beast of that bliss, not sliding now
but off your feet and running down instead
          headfirst twelve feet and how many years?

Yes, the blood stalls in your chest when you hit.
        Pines and poplars reel, crows lift from dirt,
and your father shouts a word you can't hear,
        a name, hauls the tongue out of your throat,
two knuckles on his hand shredded from bashing
        the fuel pump into place on the Olds.

This is air you breathed in me then,
        these are the things you sing through my skin,
and you are not my prison, but pure verb
        inscribed in blood, remembered to me
later by the grasp of my daughter's hand,
        by the granite slab of my father's gravestone.

I don't think we return by accident
        to such vaults, but I know better than
to call these fitful blasts of blindness
        vision—a moment's rise in the current
at best, some pebbled bedrock showing through.
        I do not bring my self here to drink.

No picture of my mind revives that much.
        I can't depend on any vagrant glimpse
to heave me back to you; yet sometimes
        even the wave of your hand will halve me,
split my circumference, knife my bitter rind.
        I see where you wave atop the ladder.

Now I'm really half-way through the woods
        and there's nothing left but memory,
that and the concave vessel of my mouth.
        We were meant to stay put, you and I,
but you are an urn of fire tipped over
        upon me—my burning, my bone-flecked ash.

2.

Eclogue

> *Now we are seated in the soft grass,*
> *Begin the singing.*
>
> —Virgil

All night we listened to Yiorgos babble:
  The golden years return, blah, blah…
    How much shit does he throw on his fields?

Crops droop. Cows slow. Dogs sag.
  Toads clog the roads. Last night's milk
    curdled in the bowl, as if my ewe's

got the evil eye, or Plusios, that scag,
  Menalcus'd her again. Only the rats grow fat.
    I wish us success and good riddance.

We've seen bodies stacked like boulders,
  men dragged like rakes, axed women. We ape
    some dream of life, aching toward what?

So we wanted to give that city the slip,
  squawk awhile out here on our fragile pipes,
    spirited by shots of rot-gut.

My torso sleeps, but my selves won't snore.
  They lumber from these groves unhinged,
    howling up the mountain like maenads.

Before we fall into our beards, Philias,
  she'll come, our Muse, shaped in the oddest garb.
    She can cure even our rancid meat.

Picture her now, making a sideways
  lurch down the hill, like that one there:
    our mono-wattled goat with the hay gut.

I love her, bucolic as she is, my
  saddest of all, Queen of some Underworld,
    eyes hunched too high, brow sunk too low.

Where she stares, I too want to go.

Eclogue 2

Between us and Etna the sky is fair,
  but the mountain smokes again.
    I maunder my way to the ossuary:

those few square feet of ash,
  skulls gashed with dents, rent by arrow-holes,
    our city mapped down to the bones.

We lack the means to move on. But the flock is fine.
  At the shore yesterday, a wind of crab husks
    and mildewed nets, gnats roiling, bladders of fish.

You came there to report a feud with Plusios,
  complained your pipe of severed reeds won't play.
    We drank some hours in sun: a wine for gods,

same as flame, tide for the tongue,
  and we spewed songs from that bad amphitheatre,
    wind blowing back our beach-breath,

moments that never happened, some that did.
  You asked how a natural sea could burn.
    There is the charred water, you point out:

a jagged calcareous ribbon wrapped
  in horizons of basalt. Deep from the sea's belly,
    I believe, such wonders are belched.

And all at once, when the lyre went quiet,
  our talk turned to lava, *demoboros*, devourer
    of property, earth's heat machine, effusive rock.

Eclogue 3 (Cyclops)

Small change, when we' are to bodies gone.
—Donne

Once naked in the shade, we bleat and buck
like any goats, spun by the dervish drone
cicadas scratch. Where there are violets
we slick the ground purple with our shoulders.
Poppies bleed curry where our heels spur earth,
a horse we lash sheepishly at first, then
faster than earth is meant to run. I hear
that word you moan—*interinanimate*—
your tongue undone by the body's Sanskrit,
a language only the eye speaks, half-closed,
a rush of pigment we're melted into
until that's all we see, our single eye.
We were schooled in the dialogue of one,
in the rank, the honey-ripe, the fertile.

Eclogue 4 (Goat Funeral)

I fled the tavern soaked with booze and gravitas,
stumbled into the scrub along the river,
cursing the whole crowd, their bouzouki kitsch,
the ardor of their mob confidence,
woke only when that shepherd Julianna
lit the pyre for her stillborn goat, wailed
against the spirit that claimed it too soon.
Understand that it was early—the grass
still slick, her firewood soggy with smoke.
The sycamores were involved with their fog.
The deer were busy hiding in the brush.
She had acacia blossoms in her braids
and I saw that a little pollen dusted
the shoulder where she'd rent her mourning shawl.
The dead one was wreathed with olive leaves,
a pile of grain uneaten at the mouth.
We made an odd society by that bank:
two humans too familiar with the dead,
the dead still waiting for someone to speak,
the wilderness around us watching,
the town behind us stupidly asleep.
What choice did I have? The goat was dead,
the girl pretty, the river risen too high.
It was for her the animal inside me
rose from its lair, shook off its winter sleep,
and I took her in my arms, and stoked the fire,
and helped her burn—oh heartless god—the little beast.

Eclogue 5

You ask me what I cannot stand, stoned as you are
  and still wanting at my bumpkin philosophy
as we stroll and stalk the masterpieces.
   If you pass the pipe I'll spill my guts. I *am* tired
of being tired, of sleeping while I'm awake.
   I even tire of light, but never of wine,
or stones carved with satyrs and plastered girls.
   I tire of coming where so much shade is wasted
on frills, diamond stuff, and precious eggwash.
   The simplest trip to town fixes me with perils
a shepherd can't find his way home from, the scam
  of syllogisms that all end the same sad way:
therefore we are mortal. That conclusion tires me.
   I'm tired of cold coffee, courtesy, culture.
I long for a pile of mud I can sink into.
   I'd bleed for a few days without speeches. I keep
a steadfast hope in things easy to believe in:
  magpies, dragonflies, the captive boots on my feet.
Needless to say, I love beauty, but tire of art.
   What, more than beauty, is so satisfied with itself?
Still, we followed Plusios to this baubled crypt
  he built to amass his exquisite trash:
each petty lie at the museum's heart brings
  the anaesthetic from which none come round to bear
upon our days—neither beauty nor truth can stall
  that last sigh we'll emit gushing eternity.
Eternity—why say more? After all the doors are slammed
  at last on tourists and schoolchildren, even this place
lets down its hair. The Madonnas start weaning their babies;
  Jesuses come down, happy for a break
from hanging. Every landscape sloughs green; every river
  comes undammed, drowning the peasants again.

14

Each dove ditches an ecclesiastic frieze. Because they were made
        to keep shut up, only the mummies won't cheer
our demise. I tire of mummies, and doves, and bleeding deity.
        I flee the flood-lit military wing: those spectacles
of god-smitten country-lovers clambering for death;
        back-lit scabbards pyxed and beautiful as jewels;
that tableau where fifteen warriors rattle marble muskets still.
        I tire of their remembered armies.
Meanwhile, while we chatter on with our symmetries
        and cornball crap, plotting ditsy dithyrambs,
the statues might hurdle from their plinths
        into combat. Angry as men, invisible as men.

Eclogue 6

You managed to swell the conversation, plying
me with grog and a platter of mushrooms.
Then I awakened to the call of Silenus,
his Thracian dirge refracted through the leaves
of a pistachio tree—each branch smoldered
while we stared, then blossomed into a swarm of eyes.

When I woke again, I thought I heard you
wish you lived farther from the world, that some
hermit wisdom epigrammed the pages of your book.
But you won't write an anchorite's healing Bible;
your dreams spring from our common trenches of ash
and graveyards greener than they have a right to be.

If I woke again, I could not hear you
since all I heard fell open like a broken gate:
I was dumbfounded by the hammering
clatter our lambs made when they plummeted to earth
—no one else could bear the semaphoric
epic they bleated out in their dying.

I woke once more when the sky's atlas
scrawled its noise on the basin of my skull
and five armies marched between us, fighting over
nothing. Three distinct excuses made them shell
the empty goat-pens, but I didn't learn them.
Their pyres singe the edges of our poetry.

Outside everything, we see as far as vultures,
what history can't, invent an anthem to survive.
Since nothing worthwhile is beyond the rise, past
the verge of our vineyard, we invite nothing in, fix it
with our cairns, with our tangled wire and fence posts,
and allow ourselves the luxury of that lie.

16

Minimalist Eclogue

for Neil and Mohini

Where are we?
      Empty pastures far and wide.
What is it?
      A system of cruelties.
What's the body for?
      To keep the beat.
Where do we find it?
      Under the mountain, deep
      inside the ear.
What is experience?
      Not anyone else.
How do we win?
      More courage having
      resolved to die.
What do we want?
      A luminarium.
And what are we?
      All sweat and spit.
What are we?
      Tufa and spume.
What are we?
      Sated with seeing.
How will we know?
      Not by chance.
When are we done?
      When no god's left standing.

Eclogue 7 (Matia)

When I lifted my eyes I saw you,
foreigner, in the shade of the fig tree.
The country welcomed you with rain.

I climbed the tree to shake its branches,
scattering magpies into the hills:
together we gathered that sticky fruit.

The orchard was quiet when you spoke
and at your word my entire body
unbound its nets: the honeycomb

and my dark honey, my strongest wine
drained to the lees. We filled a deep vessel
—yes, what ordinary beings we were

before our sap and vision made us
magicians of the flesh. Again
tonight, I went out into the city,

to the markets and ice houses,
through flooded squares and swollen streets,
seeking for you everything I love.

And as if out of nothing—Fire,
impossible flames consuming the city
—you, my eyes, exquisitely burning.

Eclogue 8 (Winter)

Pacing the hill in snow, the shot I hear
is from another hill, this blood I trace
a staggered, gut-shot deer's come from below,
the chill of such things heaving in the dusk
where even the creek has soldered to its rock.
More follow: fierce crows unstationed
east by ricochet to roost at Woodcock Dam.
These last mornings beat as hard as wings
against our stone house; a lid of rusted tin
traps the town for weeks of desperation.
Ten below. And our neighbor with his gun.

Pay attention, today's the twenty-third
of the year, risen from its six-deep tundra
to ravage our parcel of sluggish tilth.
We dig in vain among the hard, heaped banks
for the shells he chucked, find only boot-prints
and the drooled-on shreds of black cigars.
Who wants to be the thing that he hunts next?
Cold land, your punishment is our frontier:
we skim the soup from its fat, we stalk
the house, crouch when another blast rattles
shadows off the iced limbs of the valley.

Eclogue 9

Now the season comes when the birds fall,
their migrations bewildered by missiles.
They litter our lawns without saying a word.

Thus every feverish apathetic
earns cash to buy his suburban beer:
we all must keep the country clean. So much

that is common has become uncommon.
Our pastures are supernaturally
green. The dirt itself is dying of health,

pleasing only the Emperor's right eye.
From where we sit, our view is all volcano,
spurting with impossible crudeness.

The sacred bees, tired of mining essence
from thyme, swarm the public statuary
to vibrate the marble groin of Caesar.

Once, the cattle stopped chewing when we sang;
insightful goats wobbled from the mountain,
spurred by Pan and the promise of acorns.

Now that nature mocks us, we say farewell
to the oracles and caryatids
in favor of an awkward, backward bliss,

clip the hedge between dissent and despair,
no more unruly than a clutch of lambs,
yet company, somehow, to the vulgar.

Our distress is merely metaphysical,
we often wish, an inconvenience
we constitute, in spite of ourselves,

by continuing stubbornly to live.
So we pound out, with little sticks and stones,
the lewdest music: singing with our mouths shut.

Epode

Without a moment's notice, that day
      comes back to me:

we'd limped from town by foot, wine-sodden
      and blinded by lunch,

were compelled by August sun toward a pond
      we'd dreamed of—

some place beyond ourselves, at least, one you'd
      spoken of before.

I've kept you fixed there since, outlined now
      in ocher and black

on a clay drinking cup no one alive
      will ever see eyes in:

your sprawled body in the shade, a tangle
      of fern and thornapple,

the pool's besotted mirror casting
      back to shadows

that shudder of desire.

3.

Days of 1987

The exceptional thing about us
was not that we survived
on speed and weed alone,
burning textbooks to keep warm
when our slum-lord crashed the furnace.
Nor the fact that all the cops in Madison
knew us by name, were bored
by our vomiting and nudity.
And we never made any real breakthrough
in late century metaphysics,
in spite of reading Rimbaud
and staring too long into Swedenborg.
We named every kitchen cockroach
Jesse Helms, failed
all the easy classes on purpose.
We believed in garbage and guitar.
We cried a little every day to please ourselves.

Still, from here it is impossible
not to see that we left some portion
of our crass divinity hidden
under the northeast corner of the Park Street
overpass, along with some Marlboro Reds
and our spray-painted crossbones.

Dear Eternity, suppose we didn't know better.
Forgive us our trespassing and stolen beer.
Remember it was always snowing,
or about to snow, and yet
we still fell through love at least once a week,
and we still knew how to imagine
we could outlive ourselves at least.

The Blue Jay

after Montale

Some report
him an egg-thief, a gaudy
pillager of nests.

Not the one
that crashed on my garden path,
loud as a hailstorm

of sapphires.
He is no student of Kant,
though it is certain

ant-hills and
the habits of worms comprise
his metaphysics.

The human
psyche has at least two parts
and neither can fly:

we flutter
about as well as we can,
dive-bombing the moon

and every
unflappable multitude
to outlast ourselves.

He's no hawk.
His dominion is measured
in caterpillars,

his back-stretched
wings in increments of sky.
When he serenades

a sunset,
his music is pure vowel
percussed by chainsaws,

steel guitar,
and the four last songs of Strauss.
Only the jay can

plunge so deep;
the berry-shades of summer
are his; heat lightning

and six shades
of the color blue are trapped
in his marble eye;

the lost psalm
and unfinished aria,
his. Other birds can

sing in tune
but none can make their grief sound
so much like belief.

Amanita muscaria

Mornings in September, when it's too late
to bother, too late to abandon it all, I walk

the ravine, pick my poisons: wormwood, nightshade,
and those red-capped beauties blighted with white.

They wait there, deep enough to smother
me back into breath. The thing I stalk

is so close I could notch it with this spade.
A wing. Another kind of sight.

Anatomy

1. The Will

The thing's dull, but ripe with possibility:
mouse-gray, possum-tailed, reeking of whiskey,
with the natty locks of a desert prophet,

playing its trump, obeying its own harmonics.
Though cozy as the tar in your favorite pipe,
it becomes unsettled each time you stop to think.

Pick at it with your nail until it comes loose,
like a strangeness scabbed over with some sense,
an oracle husked from its need for the future.

It's the root boring into your jawbone.
You'll want another when this one's gone:
last codicil, last thing to do, last will.

2. The Pupil

No dark-prowed vessel can cleft its way deeper
than this vitriolic black, the last defense
against wonder, void and centerless as doubt.

The view from here is soiled by twaddle:
abandoned whitewalls, oil-slicked feathers,
and the erratic climate of a northern island.

This yolk is kept pickled in its own clear brine,
lolling in alabaster, bored by circumference,
yet even when it quivers the edge holds fast,

though it can bear no perspective on itself,
must survive on the inky sustenance,
what evidence it can muster sipping vastness.

3. The Pelvis

Suspended by strings, this mobile's shadow
resembles Saturn first, then a broken lyre,
and its music is nothing if not inspired,

this harbor for the out-of-body, a terminal port,
part aperture, part keel, part contact sport.
Inlet and outlet, all our eggs in one basket.

When submerged in its basin, we play a part
the sacrum decrees, hear our own heartbeat
doubled by its several, over-sized ears.

All circuitous tracts find conclusion here.

Portrait Detail, with Pear

Ants have razed the paradise of the pear,
  regiments summoned by a mighty singing
    through cracks you can't see in the floorboards.
The time was ripe for their enthusiasm,
  their sense of business and industry,
    the waving of their antennae like flags,
      their trails across the plane of formica.

The corpse will soon cave beneath its own weight.
  Its yellow hips have started to pucker,
    mottled by a few improvised brushstrokes
where the delicate skin has sugared through.
  What a shame there's no color to convey
    the exquisite perfume of this sagging.
      It's really too soggy to handle, but if

you hoist it from the saucer anyway,
  the pear hangs on, like magnet to metal,
    suctioned for a moment by what it drained
in the long hurry to decimate itself:
  this amber-colored crescent of syrup
    enriched by the carcass of one lost ant,
      last cognac of vanilla, blood and myrrh.

Portrait Detail, with Bat

In the background you feel
a spattered shadow orbit the bedroom,
just a quiver of wings
that hides in the curvature
of one ear, some corridor of sensation
swooped into, left reeling.
Then, with one inky swath,
what was just a suspicion of bat,
smears light from wall to wall.
The thing casts no shadow
but you recognize its song from your dreams,
festive as a jar of nails.
Now paint into the frame
a wife and child, a cowed watchdog,
waiting for you to act.
This is your portrait now.
What you love you fear, and you love this fear,
Defender of the brood.
The bat's wings are wide
as a gull's, with panels through which to see
darkly. It's tuned into
frequencies quieter than
the rush of your blood. You are alarmed
by what alters your image,
you are put off
by your flight from it, this beauty,
a daughter of gravity.
Yet you fetch a jar, close in.
Your ghosts watch from under the blankets
and you know it's time
to dance it to a corner,
make it finally perch, trapeezing
like a porcupine cocoon.

It chatters with you there
and the ears pull back like a Doberman's
when you meet face to face:
the bronze helmet of fur,
the limitless wells of those tiny eyes,
and you, baring your teeth.

"The World Reduced to One Thing"

—Stevens, "Adagia"

At the end of the lane a pummeled bird
or magnitudes of fact that clip our wings.
Maybe something more sinister still,
like the invalid measurement of man,
or a wave cresting under the chin, that dream
of drowning again, water churned to black.
There will be water, there will be water,
storm clouds busy from buoy to cliff.
Too much ballast and too much dross
to know transparency in this body.
Nightmares rise in the harbor: tides,
nothing beyond life's usual freight.
Just some trawling out beyond the bank.
Our knowledge. Our killick. Our gangplank.

4.

Duet with Fernando Pessoa

At times we wish that we could disappear,
having followed too long the terrified trails of sparrows
between rafter beams and the branches of elms
—all that's been dashed upon itself
in back alleyways and coal-pits, everything I follow
· on my brainless ramble through the market,
where I flatten out to fit the tatters of my wallet.
Meanwhile, the baker's fire collapses back to ash,
and the broad-chested church on the corner
absorbs all sounds not sanctioned by the rain.

When we see between things, where ether's heaving
at the border, see how the shape of the leaf, for instance,
dilates beyond contours permitted by the eye,
where underlying matter can muster beyond
the banter of books, then we see a votive geometry
known only to those versed in my Jesuit liturgy of the senses,
a new music swelling the topsails of the altar-boys' tongues.
Meanwhile, the same atomic fog,
and madmen thrash the congas of our garbage pails.

I see between things, through the narrow chinks,
through a negative space even knowing can't fill,
through a neon hum the insects master to pester us;
I surrender the hub of skin that's strung me out,
slack as an old tire, the forehead having tasted exterior
it forgot was there, my mind left back in its neoclassical urn.
And I'll have more wine, if that's all I think can happen,
and I'll have more wine, if life is nothing,
brimming as I drink it with gypsy ventriloquism,
noting, as I down it, my duty to the voices I must dream.

Duet with Czeslaw Milosz

(1911-2004)

In my tavern, by my sea, the tables grow unstable,
overburdened by half-finished plates, demitasse,
and the elbow-weight of sacred conversation,
for which even time will stall its manic gyroscope.
I am content to doubt that anything beyond this
has substance. These slate shingles will never fail,
nor the cheap silverware, burnished in spite of itself,
nor, like a thing correspondent to the waves, your voice.
As if the balancing of glasses in the air could steady us,
as if the olive tree rooted next to this table was ballast
for our confidence in wood, and wine, and being here.

Duet with D.H. Lawrence

There is no port, there is nowhere to go...

It's true, we'll skulk away
in little boats, equipped
with death's cuisine.

Bad paddlers we're destined
to be, crabbing circles,
our bodies fermenting like fruit.

No bed, no silk, no pillow.
Our souls are heavy with tallow.
The valley threatens to flood.

And where the forest parts,
a little church where torments
breed: a pretty gang of seizures,

ten soldiers in blindfold,
a ferryman casting off from shore.
And flaking from the farthest wall,

Christos Elkomenos,
a pale, pale Jesus, undone by pain.
And all the while our bodies

hum their thumpy tunes.
Our little lamps are lit
and snuffed, and lit again.

Between choruses of us and air,
the honey breath of summer
holds, barricades the door.

Blues for Bill Matthews, Dead at 55

Tonight I scavenge your lyrics, famished
for more of their erudite monologue,
but I get only gossip of garlic,

a little chatter in the pan,
rumors of where you cook now,
cup of fire in hand, while you improvise

courses for the Belly and Mind.
Did you hear? They say you're literature.
And surely it's packed with poets down there,

that circle where we Epicureans fry
our feeble meat. What does a palate
like yours make of the final vintage?

I toast hilarity's posterity, wonder if we
might still catch you dreaming of saxophones
along the wide 52nd Streets of Hell.

That search party you first dispatched, Bill,
has returned much too soon, leaving us
this banquet of your slow-cooked jazz.

Violin Solo

For SFJ

We must allow ourselves music at least,
      an hour alone with the calculus of Bach,
a little concentration, just one side
      of one record, one chapter, one poem.
We must permit ourselves some fever,
      some fire, more light to see the dead we grieve,
enough to leave the dead we grieve alone.
      The bow is content with its ration of rosin.
The books can bear this weight on their spines.
      Again we'll know octave, scale, arpeggio.
Again ships, stars, lightning, a horizon.
      Again clear-eyed constellations, night.
We must allow ourselves music at least.

Parenthesis

Monteverdi there, a background
purpled by mezzo soprano,
and other thoughts lifting
like incense from the metered lines
of open books. Even the cat,
my Dionysian prowler,
once a marauder of all light,
is afire with concentration
where she's dying on the kilim.
On the table, cut for nothing,
a lemon flaunts its open wounds.

Paul Celan

You muted the unearthly trumpet blasts,
heard syllables beyond us, death's music
in a landscape where books and people lived
but refuse to return, no longer knowing
the tongue: bruised fruit in rotten mouths.
No one failed to see what was left behind,
interred beneath blizzards of arsenic
where nothing grows, dwells, or is ever saved.
Shades flee in formation, forgetters,
seeking shelter in lies and doubts,
though documents persist, multiplying.
Telling it now lifts no refrain to you,
poet, drowned somewhere among the rest.
It is time now to retrace that dying.

Duet with Salvatore Quasimodo

When I die I'll meet you at Mycenae
where stones mark out an alphabet of spoils,
leaving only a few square facts unquarried.

You'll remember the place by its painting:
a splash of Sicilian green, cypresses,
and a pointillism of widow's heads.

The murmurs of every Medieval square
give in to dusk; iron church bells
brim with the ether you leave in your wake.

Take down your lyre from the willow now,
it has sheltered long enough, like a flea
in the sultan's beard, your island music

with its ancestry in the sea itself,
seasoned with a cloud-burst from Malta,
and cannon dust, and bruised acacia blossoms.

Show me how to call beyond vacancy,
since we cannot out-sing the megaphones;
when we become famished by that prattle

sustenance will be waiting for us there,
concealed by shadows in a beehive tomb
where the dead mount their chariots for war.

5.

Purgatory, a Postcard

I ate octopus with a survivor tonight.
We slammed vodka, compared tattoos.
His added up to ninety, so I paid.
Beyond that, there's not much company.
I attend the hangings. The library
isn't half bad. I try not to complain.

Thank you for your gifts: the shredded documents,
the hammers, that crate of artichokes.
We tried to plant the corpses you sent,
but the ground is much too hard for digging.

I'm writing you this postcard so you know.
Please give my regards to the President.

Though it's much colder here than one expects,
things are, I must say, awfully beautiful.

Detail from *The Martyrdom of San Mauricio*, El Greco

Some things are not meant to please the King,
though soldiers do parade in pretty armor:
contrapposto, they dance almost on point,
halberds and banners erect as we'd expect.
The Cretan, Domenikos Thetokopoulos,
perceives the martyrdom of Mauricio
as a jagged stump usurped by blossoms.
Elsewhere, as always, some bloody trunk is sprawled
before its circus of prickly penitents.
Even the orchestra of angels, surfing cloud,
blares the saint to death. Their thunderstorm
rumbles on without his notice in some sky.
Nor can he feel the earth beneath his feet
where lilies split stone, some buds unopened.

Coleridge in Valletta

Thirty drops in a warm tumbler of lemonade
flood, for now, a cavern the Speedwell ripped open.
Three nights his dreams glisten with constellations.
Then, like ink diffused in water, the fever fades.
Their Arabic afflicted with Italian,
Maltese maids attend him patiently,
barking mongrel platitudes. Each morning at ten
they drag a sofa beneath the laurel trees
so he suffers a pen and paper for hours.
I took no dose, he writes. Then does. Some miseries
are subtler still—in the governor's garden
he sinks in open air, surfaces to see
unearthly leaves, a pomegranate in flower, and
everywhere, murmuring with bees, the poppies.

Azaleas

from Milies to Tsangarada, Pelion

Always moving, with villages
fly-specked across the local map,
each boasting a profound new jam,
museums we'd rather not see,
and some destitute chestnut trees
making shade for a famous square.

Every square has been footnoted,
so we must see them all, in cars
liberated from rental lots.
Everything we claim is rented:
our spiffy mountain house, these wheels.
It's all impermanent and strange.

And every road from here to there
was no doubt made to murder us,
each turn a sheared-off mountainside
impressed with shrine and crucifix
by someone who died, or didn't.
Beyond that, mist and quiet air,

edges we want to peer over
since somewhere below is the cove
we're driving for, with its promise
of simple wine and salt water.
Each switchback leads us deeper in:
shade, shade, then the predictable

sun-blitzed curve blasted from its rock
veering out again toward nothing.
Around one turn a gravel pile,

men willing their cement to dry.
Around another, battered trucks.
The shops are shut. Churches are locked.

Still we harden to it, grip down,
unfold the map another square,
tempered by the ordinary
fact of gravity, those moments
of clarifying emptiness
toward which we must steer, then swerve from.

What marks the shoulder between there
and asphalt, what absolves the air—
these defiant, raging clusters
of cream and blood-ripe azaleas
pitching like crowds of burning wings
we don't have the guts to follow.

Our eyes grow sick of blossoming;
we long to shut them and move on,
ourselves exhausted in peak bloom,
five stamens bowing down each head,
deep-rooted things, clutching at cliff,
since they have nowhere else to go.

Late Adam Thinking

The days are elegant and dull
The nights cool and sexual

When clouds come   you play piano and make
martinis while I sew

When the moon fattens   you smoke on the lawn
sprinklers going

There is ganja spilled in the shag
a pitcher of tomato juice in the fridge

The ceiling fan rotates   rotating slowly

You say   this comedy of atoms
forms itself in circular things

I try to understand   with words
but only vowels come

Days pass
Nights pass

Now I find you locked in
the closet eating onion
after onion
acerbic reptile shedding skins

But even this late there are a thousand
reasons to remember our songs
this late
we could manage a samba in the garden

First Objects

... unstoried, artless, unenhanced.

The moment we set off on the ocean,
steering pine boxes with nothing but faith,
we became ideas, the bas–relief
of an army the gods set in motion,
hardened with an integument of gold.
Dandelion, limestone, free enterprise.
A hurricane of glass beads and horseflies.
Things we believed at the dreadful thresholds
of canyons. All too grand. Steeple, chimney,
tower, sky: erections proved our destiny
to contract the size of the hemisphere.
We might have stayed put, but couldn't bear
the sense that we were rising, calm as geese
caught between the sights of a shotgun.

Ohio Elegy

I drive too fast with Cleveland
behind me, past stadiums and thirteen zip codes,
through rigid and red-blooded suburbs at dusk.
And instead of drinking
in the highway, its light-scattering steeples
and that mass of starlings released
like an unclenched fist from a line of hedges
I can't see, I'm thinking again of my country:
gray factories snoring outside Painesville
and the meat-packing plants of Ashtabula
—the one sow I imagine there,
scratching her bristled ass along that last steel chute
like the torturer's horse in Auden,
penned up in my mind tonight
with a hundred other agonies,
not the very least of them redeeming us.

I speak too plainly here.
Such honesty betrays my desire to suffer silence
silently. I think of all the men
scuffling, somewhere, into concrete bunkers.
I think of Whitman patching the pulped arms of soldiers;
of James Wright humming Vallejo in Martin's Ferry.
I think of something that makes me resent the passage of time,
or the plain sense of passing here:
the greasy shanks of warehouse loading docks,
and haloed wrecks in truck stop parking lots,
and rabbits darting deeper into night.
I'm steering my way out of this day.
The fields of Ohio are giving up too,
slumped fences and stubble now briefly lit
when a phalanx of Hell's Angels
ratchets down the left lane

busting up the monotony
of a road already exhausted
from waiting so long to wail.

Ariadne (Postscript)

The story of my marriage is all bunk,
      though Titian paints it best: the hunky god,
his parade of horny drunks and goat boys
      come to fetch me. Truth be told, I liked him,

that god, in spite of how I lost myself.
      Such bombast for a simple girl from Crete.
Rumors of my death are also too easy
      —happy endings were not my specialty

so Bacchus spun some stars? Gibberish.
      Here's how it really went: I did it myself
swimming with a rock strapped to my waist.
      Forgive me such an operatic end.

The language I heard was never my own.
      I was groped at the market; I endured
the jealousy of village women.
      And always some man or bull ready to rut.

Finches and stray dogs were my companions,
      the only things that would not flee from me.
When I drift back home at last from Naxos
      I'll fetch the stone that weighed me back to life.

Last Words from Elpenor

Bewildered by the scent of clotted blood
and the clatter we dead made drinking it,
I heaved up to the sewer where you stood,
cursed you, master, a swine who would forget
son, wife, home, and me—this last betrayal
most appalling: we all must bury friends.
The mast of my neck snapped on Aeaea,
I want to say. You left me. In the end
we are forbidden to close our eyes
and must watch our beloved lives slip
back down ladders we worked so long to climb.
Sailor, you too will lose your famous grip.
Before you go, chuck me a single oar.
May I be cool beneath these sycamores.

Aegean: Flight 652

The names of seashore towns run out to sea...
—Elizabeth Bishop

That could be Paros, I say, though I know
its body only from maps: the blunt head,
two rabbit-ear peninsulas, the port.

You've already recognized Naxos,
its marble gate to the invisible
just beyond the town, all the ragged beads

of western bays where you floated, pregnant,
five whole days the last time we were here.
This year, above the thrum of two loud props,

our daughter babbles her own geography
in a tongue we haven't managed to learn.
A heavy diaper since the airport, Rhodes,

she tantrums in the crowded seat until
you point out the window, islands below.
Mykonos. Tinos. Andros. A dragon's tail.

Delos: discarded pit of an olive.
We taught her how to point and so she points,
translates all we say into her single vowels:

karpouzi   thalassa   petaloudes
Just yesterday we held her high enough
into the shadowed mane of a gum tree

to fill her infant gaze with butterflies:
a hundred thousand crowded to a tree
in a valley of a hundred thousand trees.

Below us now, the Aegean churns
like a sea of wings, waves bucking skyward.
There's no place for her eyes to land, or ours.

Would we know home from here if we saw it?
Is it the water that makes us forget?
Yet the names of islands gestate in us

long after the Atlantic has replaced
this region where the glasses are always full
and the world is all whitewash, whitewash.

It is possible to believe in this.
We have supposed it lucky to be born,
as Whitman says we must. No ordinary faith

but an open-winged longing for more
love, deeper than our island solitudes.
So we announce for her everything we see:

words are flesh and blood we can devour
since in time they become what we're made of.
Another year we'll climb Thera's gnarled spine,

go where the half-moon of Chios eyes Izmir
and Lesbos opens its ear to the sea.
Spetses. Hydra. Poros. Aegina.

The world is too full, never time enough
or words—we're even out of water now,
Athens coming into view. She gives up

the window for your breast until we land.
So many islands, so much blessed salt,
this feast we could not finish by ourselves.

About the Author

Christopher Bakken is also the author of *After Greece*, for which he received the T.S. Eliot Prize in Poetry in 2001, and he is co-translator of *The Lions' Gate: Selected Poems of Titos Patrikios* (2006). His poems, essays, reviews and translations have appeared widely, in *The Paris Review, PN Review (U.K.), Raritan, Gettysburg Review, Literary Imagination, Contemporary Poetry Review, Agni,* and elsewhere. He divides much of his time between Greece and Meadville, Pennsylvania, where he lives with his wife, Kerry Neville Bakken, and his two children, Sophia and Alexander. He teaches at Allegheny College.